CL

When
Parents
Split
Up...

Yvonne Johnson

For Christian
who started it all

First published 2012
by Finding The Rainbow Publishing
1

Yvonne Johnson asserts the moral right to be
identified as the author of this work

A catalogue record of this book is available from the
British Library

ISBN 978-0-9572508-0-2

Printed and bound by Short Run Press Ltd

For adults sharing this book with a young person there are notes at the back of the book to help you.

There are many young people who have contributed to the creation of this book. Some of them found the experience of their parents splitting up very upsetting and difficult.
Eventually things became more settled again, although very different.
These young people were keen to help others still making the journey.

So in this book you will hear the voices of many of the young people I have worked with, and as they wished, I have not added details that might identify them.

When

Parents

Split

Up...

Yvonne Johnson

We'd like to help you through a difficult time if we can.

Things are more settled for us now.

We've shared some of the things we felt and thought when our parents split up. You will see that lots of the things you are finding difficult were the same for us.

At one time or another we have all
felt a mix of emotions. We have
felt:

frightened,   confused,
alone, worried,   guilty
tired,   upset,   angry,
relieved, sad,
unhappy.

I'm scared. What will happen to me?

Was it my fault?

I'm so angry. Why did it have to happen to us?

I want my dad back. I don't want him to leave us.

Sometimes our parents argued and shouted.
It was very frightening.

I wish they'd stop shouting.

Do you think it'll be OK? They're always arguing.

There were times, with all
the arguing, when we got
upset and wondered if our
parents still loved us.

When our parents
first split up some of us were afraid
it might be our fault. We were
afraid we had done something to
make it happen.

Eventually we learnt that it wasn't anything to do with us. Some of us had to ask lots of adults before we could believe it really wasn't our fault.

In the end we understood we aren't responsible for making our parents happy together.

We worried about what would

happen to us.

We kept hoping things would go
back to normal.

If only they'd get back together and not argue, we could pretend it never happened.

Most of us wanted our parents to get back together again. Some of us even tried to make it happen.

> I really liked it when we all went out together for my birthday. Mum and Dad seemed to get on well and didn't argue at all.

But it never seemed to work and we had to get used to our parents living in separate places.

Lots of us were really angry about
the break up of our family.

I'm so angry.
It's not fair.

I don't want my parents
to split up. I want things
to stay how they were.

Everything is messed up
now. Why is this happening?

At one time or another lots of us worried about whether our parents would be all right on their own.

Mum's always getting upset, even when little things go wrong.

Dad doesn't seem very organised. He keeps forgetting things.

At first it was hard living with just
one parent.
Sometimes we didn't feel like we
got enough attention.

21

Gradually we got used to living with one parent, and found ways to make our new, smaller family work again.

After a while our lives were less unhappy and we began to feel better.

For some of us our new way of life included visiting our other parent. For others it didn't.

Some of us have stayed with just one parent; for others new step families have come along.

We're all glad the splitting up is over now.
It was very hard for everyone.

We live in different families now. Some of us just live with our mums. Some of us have step mums and dads. Some of us have step brothers and sisters.

Our families are all sizes and ages. It doesn't matter as long as we have a place to call "home" where we are comfortable.

Our lives have changed now and our families are different but we still have fun and enjoy ourselves.

I'm going dancing next week.

I love staying with friends.

We're going on holiday next year.

I'm going rock climbing with school next term.

My thanks go to all those who have contributed to the making of this book. To the many children and young people who have been brave enough to share their concerns and fears, and to the parents and carers who have allowed their children to share quite private parts of their lives with a total stranger.

Thank you too to all those others who continue to support this work and have helped to get this book into print.
You have all been amazing!

Yvonne

Reading this book together:
Children and young people might like to read this alone, or share it with someone they trust.

It usually works best if that person is a trusted adult friend or professional rather than a parent, so that feelings can be shared openly without upsetting the parent.

If a child or young person has asked you to share this book with them, what is important is that you:
- listen and try to understand
- ask any questions gently
- don't try to "fix" things, or tell them how you see it
- don't take offence (see opposite page)
- accept the feelings they have, whatever they are.

Our feelings change over time, and can be very intense and raw when major change takes place. In that situation, it can be difficult to express how we feel at all, and it can be easy to offend people when we try.

Looking back, we sometimes see things differently, but at the time, the important thing is to feel that it's "ok" to feel the way we do for as long as we need to.

The most difficult, but also most common emotion to deal with is anger. It is quite normal and healthy. Everyone is different and some may handle it well. Others may need help to express it or manage it.

If you need more information please go to www.findingtherainbow.co.uk

Finding the Rainbow Publishing was set up to publish books that help children and young people meet the challenges they face as they grow up.

"When Parents Split Up..." supports the children and young people affected by their parents splitting up or getting divorced. It aims to reduce isolation and to give supportive adults a starting point for engaging with those affected, so that they can share how they feel with someone they trust.

Support materials and training in using this book are also available if required.
For further information please go to:
www.findingtherainbow.co.uk